73

*Learn Then Burn 2: This Time It's Personal*

ॐ

edited by Tim Stafford

Write Bloody Publishing
*America's Independent Press*

Austin, TX

**WRITEBLOODY.COM**

Learn Then Burn 2: This Time It's Personal

© 2014 Write Bloody Publishing
No part of this book may be used or performed without written consent from the
author, except for critical articles or reviews.

Write Bloody
First Edition
**ISBN: 9781938912504**

Cover art by Ashley Siebels
Proofread by Andie Flores, Helen Novielli, and Heather Knox
Interior layout by Ashley Siebels
Edited by Tim Stafford
Author photo by Uwe Lehmann


Type set in Bergamo from www.theleagueofmoveabletype.com

Printed in Tennessee, USA

Write Bloody Publishing
Austin, TX
Support Independent Presses
writebloody.com

To contact the author, send an email to writebloody@gmail.com

MADE IN THE USA

*LEARN THEN BURN 2: THIS TIME IT'S PERSONAL*

*For Mikey*


*For the staff and students*
*of the West 40 Regional Safe Schools.*

# LEARN THEN BURN 2
# THIS TIME IT'S PERSONAL

# PREFACE

*For the Teachers:*

The mission of the Learn then Burn series is simple: put high quality, accessible poetry into the hands and heads of students and teachers. This is not meant to replace the classics, but to be used in addition to. Maybe this is a bridge to those poems. Maybe this book is your curriculum. That's up to you. We know how hard it can be to get kids to connect with poetry and we want to break down the barriers. We want it so that poetry becomes a natural part of your class as opposed to something you have to teach in April that bores you and your class to death. This is a resource that has already been used successfully in classrooms from the South side of Chicago to rural Mongolia. We know you'll find the best way to use it.

*For the non-teachers:*

See that paragraph up there? Don't read it. This is a rad book filled with rad poets who wrote rad poems. That's all you need to know!

# LOVE WITHOUT LIMIT, QUESTION, HOWL FOR ME (CANAANITES)

by Nick Weaver

I saw the best minds of my generation destroyed by
news feeds, direct messages, and status updates,
hysterically dragging themselves through the cyber streets at dawn,
begging for a retweet, they scream staccato keystrokes like Facebook
junkies.

Us Instagram hipsters are hashtag angry and hashtag hungry
Us gamers go wild for hits of Mountain Dew Code Red,
the bacchanalian love found during a Warcraft raid,
hypnotized by our avatars, our keyboards are STD free
but our porn soaked-minds define scenes
our parents didn't want to.

Because we are lonely for someone to check our check ins,
be the 2nd 3rd and 4th parties in our Foursquares
because we want you to know where we are
and we want you to like us and like us for liking you,
and we want you to notice when we're not at home.

I saw the eyes of my peers turn dark, dimmed from an app store glow,
they Draw Something until they
exhaust the ink supplies in their fingertips
they play Words with Friends until they have neither.

We stopped sacrificing to Moloch
after children became the Canaanites,
the fire gods lace themselves between the notches in our spines,
we build funeral pyres for reality TV,
and we bleed for Greenwood when we write our blog posts,
but we can't call that blood our own.

Because on every street in every suburb
you will find us among the front lawns,
watching the stars, searching for something red in the sky
because it's been so long since we've seen something truly red,
it's been so long since something red has belonged to us and not the
neighborhood,
that we can't even lay claim to the history in our veins anymore.

Because I wonder where the rebels have gone.

Because I wonder where the stories have gone,
and the Canaanite memories,
and the Byzantine laughs,
and the breakfasts you didn't feel the need to document.

Because really we don't want you to listen to our quotes,
or our reviews,
we want you to listen to our howls.
We want you to scroll down to the comments section of our youth,
and reply to all the questions left unanswered,

And open up "an epilogue of our lives dot tumblr dot com,"
and it will be free for anyone to follow,
and one day in the future,
it won't be full of all the words we never said
but the explosive TNT
of a million voices you've never heard before.

I wanna detonate my online presence
and leave the trench that I dug in my browser behind,
I wanna join my generation in deleting our eHarmony profiles,
and find love with someone who I can be a monster with.

4

Because I want to be a werewolf, a pack animal
I want to join my brothers' DNA,
cursing and foaming at the mouth,
we will tear into the chests and rip open the hearts
of anyone who will bare them to us,
and we'll find passion and compassion,
we'll find the battlefield and the beachhead,
we will find the stories again,
and we will lift them up to the cosmos,
dripping and wet, clenched between our jaws,
we will show our pain to the world and we will show the world they still
have heroes.

Because there's a full moon coming,
and it's gonna be blood red.
So howl for me.

# HOW I REMEMBER IT

by Jon Sands

Second period Geometry Allison Friedman
asks about an English presentation
due sixth period worth twenty-five percent
of my grade and zero percent even started.
I begin by closing my eyes only slightly.
I do everything I would normally do, just
noticeably slower until Mr. Boyle, my teacher,
has to ask if something is wrong. I say,
*No Mr. Boyle. Not yet.*

By American History I am walking with a new
hunch in my back. I slowly run into a desk
then a person. My frown like an upside-down
whatever. By Physics, Zack Pyretzky
is carrying my backpack. I tell my teacher,
Mrs. Parrot, that, *My stomach is troubled.*
*That if I sprint from class unexpectedly,*
*It's no disrespect. But I'm going to try*
*to rough it, Mrs. Parrot. I didn't become*
*Secretary of the Student Council*
*by not roughing it.*

Twenty minutes, I break for the hallway. Cheeks puffed
sprinting through the second floor of Sycamore High School.
I smack the bathroom door with both hands.
No one is inside but *still* I rush for the stall.
I can feel crevices of the small tile floor
against my knees. My mouth open,
my body attempting to throw up
anything. I am making throaty noises,
spitting into my reflection in the water.

The nurse will be a sympathetic pushover.
My mother is at work until six.
Mrs. Wilkerson will have to pick me up
from the office and assist me out to her minivan
just as my English teacher, Mrs. May,
calls up the first presentation. Mrs. May
is the only person who will not believe me.
Her hands cast a choleric spell
as she tells me I can't just charm
and squeak my way through life.

But there I am: indignant and righteous.
In tears I storm from her classroom still clutching
a bright yellow pass that reads *Excused Absence.*
Committed to the work I have done. Full of wrath
that anyone could look at me and see
a liar.

# RANT ON WHY I HATE CURSIVE

by Dan "Sully" Sullivan

My 5th grade teacher Ms. Blanz
was a rabid Medusa of a woman.
The white strands of her hair were snakes
with red ink fangs ready
to sink into my homework.
She scared me so much
I hated learning.
She demanded the "S"
I round in my last name
resemble less a figure eight
and more of a tilted hourglass.
I wanted to tell her in 1992
we use clocks
and if her old butt wants an hourglass
she could pull one
out of the wrinkles in her face.
During my cursive lesson
Mr. Harrington's class had a pizza party
for Mike Fischer's birthday.
Ms. Blanz didn't allow pizza or cake
which sucks
because all I wanted was a cake
in the shape of a pizza
made out of frosting
with a pizza on top.
No 10 year-old wants
wheat crackers and fig spread
during the celebration of their birth.
On Halloween
Mike Fischer dressed up as Batman.
Ahmad Porter went as Freddy Krueger.

The entire school marched around
the building in order of classroom.
It was a grade school red carpet
with parental paparazzi
but the cameras stopped
when Ms. Blanz's 5th grade class strolled by
dressed as puns
representing countries of the world.
Kyle Monty was Thailand
and wore 100 ties.
Billy Rutkowski was Turkey
and dressed as a Turkey.
He was dumb (and later went to prison).
Swantice Taylor was Germany.
She painted green spots all over her body.
They were 'Many Germs'.
I was Greece dressed in a garbage can.
Get it? Greece? Grease Can??? Hilarious.
My mom wrote "Grease Can"
across the front in magic marker
for any idiot who didn't get why

I looked like Oscar the Grouch
getting off an international flight.
Blanz made us include 5 facts
about our country on our costume:
1) Population: just under 11 million.
2) Highest mountain: Mt. Olympus
3) Capital: Athens
4) Ms. Blenz ruined my 10th birthday
5) She also managed to ruin Halloween
6) I know there was only supposed to be 5
but she was a terrible math teacher
7) I just wanted to dress up
as a frickin' Ninja Turtle

and get my Skittle on
but instead I hate cursive,
hate fig spread,
hate Mr. Harrington,
hate all of Greece
except for saganaki,
and the moral of the story
is Ms. Blanz effing sucks
and she is the reason
I got arrested for spray painting
on the Dairy Queen dumpster
"Cursive is for A-Holes."

# ON THE DISCOMFORT OF BEING IN THE SAME ROOM
# AS THE BOY YOU LIKE

by Sarah Kay

Everyone is looking at you looking at him.
Everyone can tell. He can tell. So you
spend most of your time not looking at him.
The wallpaper, the floor, there are cracks
in the ceiling. Someone has left a can of
iced tea in the corner, it is half-empty,
I mean half-full. There are four light bulbs
in the standing lamp, there is a fan. You
are counting things to keep from looking
at him. Five chairs, two laptops, someone's
umbrella, a hat. People are talking so you
look at their faces. This is a good trick. They
will think you are listening to them and not
thinking about him. Now he is talking. So
you look away. The cracks in the ceiling are
in the shape of a whale or maybe an elephant
with a fat trunk. If he ever falls in love with
you, you will lie on your backs in a field
somewhere and look up at the sky and he will
say, Baby, when I die, I'm going to put a new
constellation up there so that you will know
it is for you and you will say, Baby, I already
put one, it is an elephant with a fat trunk and
sometimes it is a whale, and he will not know
what you mean but he will love you anyway.
He is asking a question now and no one has
answered it yet. So you lower your eyes from
the plaster and say, the twenty-first, I think,

and he smiles and says, oh, cool and you
smile back, and you cannot stop your smiling,
oh you cannot stop your smile.

# KISSY KISSY

by Jessica Helen Lopez


His mother gifted him the name Robert
meaning bright flame and keeper of fire
We just called him Bubba –
eloquence certainly not the average sixth-grader's finest trait

a skinny boy like a live wire and skin the color
of ten melted caramels atop a warm television set
he owned a head full of ink black curls kinky and coiled
tight as the tiny fingers I once saw etched
into a Japanese woodblock print
*The Great Wave Off Kanagawa* –

reaching little ringlets like a slow-moving halo aglow
soft like sea foam

he smelled of Jojoba and summer evening on the porch

He liked me sure enough – called me *his* woman,
my sixth-grade hips but only a slight jumprope
tremor beneath my yellow picture day dress.

It was the season for distraction
trapezoids and hypotenuse angles like knees bent
an upside down photobooth face from the monkey bars
all toothy smile and desert dry hair

the air tinkled with the silver bells
of the ice cream truck that
slowly circled round and
round our playground
like an eager shark

Bubba asked me to meet him
during second recess behind the kissing tree
and I would have if only
just to see the amber flame of his eyes
lashes long and spider soft
curled upward like a girl

He waited with his entourage of
kickballers and sixth-grade romantics
It was the historic kiss that never was.

The cottonwood was afloat that day
seed like muted firefly or snow
or furry white boats that coasted and
caught the breeze to tickle my nose

I was perfecting the cherrybomb
from the top rung of the jungle gym
scratching marks into the sand
where my gangly legs met the dirt

It was simple as math.  As clean
as an Even-Steven four-square match.
No bones about it.

Twirling round and round
in the clouds miles above
earth and then leaping like
fireball into the air – Queen of my own
Queendom for those last precious
fourteen minutes and forty-two seconds

forty-one seconds
forty seconds
of second recess

I was not the kisser of boys.
Nobody's hipless woman.
No make-believe wife
playing house behind the Maple tree.

Kissy Kissy McKisser face
in front of a squealing
pre-pubescent congregation
the scent of lunch milk
rolling in hot waves
from their collective breath

Instead I was song in motion – leopard
print trapeze artist all glitter and glow
"The Most Marvelous Magnanimous
Lady Gymnast" there ever lived!

A dare-devil aerialist
performing one-arm plange
swingover –
a vertical spectacle
like a case of silver knives
flung through the air
a frothy Magnolia
scenting my hair

I was Barbette the Enigma,
El Nino Farini and The Flying Zedoras
Lily Leitzel of the Leamy Ladies,
wings taped to my back
clad in off-the-rack discount
knock-off high-top Converse

The undisputed star prima-donna
of the triple somersault,

Thank you VERY MUCH,
Your Majesty!

I was Cherry Bomb,
Spider Monkey Dash
Kick Flip Forward
Flop and Scratch
Mark Dismount

but
      most
TRIUMPHANTLY
         and
    GLORIOUSLY
      of
            all

I was free.
I was free.
I was free.

# DOUGH

by Nate Marshall


rummaging through pockets
we put together some
ragged collection of coins
to equal a dollar or close.

walking down 47th
on streets lined
with our possible selves
selling themselves.

we arrive every afternoon,
the café, corner of king drive.

the guy who worked there
hands lamar a crossaint,
day old at best.

lamar cracks it open,
hands me half.

even week old hard bread
still melts in our mouths.

we ate and were
full (barely).

we, two rappers with
nothing but the bread
on our minds.

# GHETTO YOUTHS

by natasha carrizosa


this poem
will be written red
for the ghetto youths
that carry bricks in their bellies
because they swallowed
disregard deceit disrespect
dis poison
our children are sent out into the world to roam
with a pocket full of metaphors and moans
under a concrete tree
they dream revolution
so they revolt
with firesticks and hope
that babylon burns slow
redemption is a must

this poem
will be written red
for the ghetto youths
that run before they crawl
and crawl when they cannot stand
war awaits in the backyard
free rides on the pale horse
the politicians promise
but first
they must play warrior
sticks and stones to break their bones
but guns and bombs to kill them
a man is made but once
but children come a dime a million
freedom is a must
this poem
will be written red

for the ghetto youths
that paint their faces
defile their temples
to play palace with tainted kings
an abandoned ruin
left to raise a nation
to suffer with swollen belly
and choke on silver lining lust
repatriation is a must
this poem
will be written red
for the ghetto youths
of kingston tivoli gardens
the concrete jungle of jamaica
brick city
the boogie down
way down south
these divided states of america
sudan
somalia
ethiopia
rwanda
mama africa
juarez
guanajuato
el distrito
mexico
lithuania
kosovo
vilna
warsaw
baghdad
mosul
fallujah
this poem is written
this poem is red
red/read
for the ghetto youths

# THE YEAR MY BROTHER STOPPED LISTENING TO HIP-HOP

by Hanif Abdurraqib

I was 19
& four girls went missing
from the rusted swingset beside scottwood elementary
where we used  to throw basketballs at the bent
rim with no net after dark
& Trenton
who was once young & stole
kisses from high school girls
underneath the Bishop Hartley bleachers
got arrested for pulling
a .45 in the club because it was Saturday night &
the *N* word crawled out
from behind the wrong tongue &
swam through the bass right before the beat
dropped & someone always gotta throw fists
into something sacred after last call
& it was still eastside
& *we still so hood*
& Jay-Z called himself *Hova*
twelve times in one song
which blared from the speakers in my first apartment
so loudly I couldn't hear my father when he asked why
I didn't come to the mosque anymore
& I got a ticket for my window tint being too dark
& maybe my skin bearing too much of a resemblance on
a backstreet in Bexley but I lied & told my grandmother
it was for speeding so that I could stay fly
& my new nephew howled into the world on the same day
Biggie would have turned 30 so I was late
to the hospital because it was almost summer in the Midwest

& *mo' money mo' problems* was on the radio at sunset &
I was cruising
down Livingston with a girl riding shotgun who woke up
that morning in my Tribe Called Quest t-shirt hoping
I would finally tell her I loved her
back
& two months later she fell in love with
a coast
where my phone calls were no longer currency
& I didn't know how to define *that kind of* alone
so that year I spent my tuition refund check on new headphones that
drowned out everything

# JOY
by Laura Yes Yes

*for Khary*


I'm chasing an ice cream truck in high holy
want, blaring at the top of my lungsful for
Chipwiches, but craving a snow cone, really,
not plastic-wrapped, but the kind scraped
scooped and fresh-soaked with color, really
saturated color, dripping like a little mango,
seriously new-fallen mango, impatient to
shudder totally free from its skin, like me some
days, a little round sun to swallow, really that's
what I want, to swallow the sun, I want it
burning the perfect into me, a dart of diabolical
beauty, yes I want it inside me, I want it really
and truly enough to run wailing down the road
from bottom to top, oh darling, ice cream
trucker, mine oh mine I want it, I'm coming for
you for real I'm after my joy.

# SIXTEEN WAS THE YEAR

by Victor Infante

when I stopped throwing punches –
    when I realized the force on my bones
    equaled the force inflicted
by quick-trigger knuckles.

when I fell in love with girls whose names
    I can't recall, whose smiles echoed
rib to rib until my chest near-exploded.

when I bought "The Story of the Clash"
    and played it on my Sony Walkman
until the tape wore thin and snapped.

when I first kissed a stranger
    in the back of someone else's car;
    red-locked girl with runner's legs
    and gin on her lips.

when I bought a Ferlinghetti book
    and read it in one sitting.

when I lied about not remembering
    crashing my mother's car; not admitting
that I'd wondered, for a moment,
how the impact would ricochet
throughout my body.

when  my mistakes
    dyed their hair blue.

# SKATEBOARDERS SEE THE WORLD THROUGH A WIDE ANGLE LENS

by Tim Stafford

Wide eyes on seven-plys
see the world with a broader range of vision
The cops, suits, security guards, and tourists
can all see but they'll
never understand

Mr Mayor, please
don't get mad at these kids
Get mad at your architects and developers
for their inviting over-use of marble
and negative space

Mr Mayor, please
don't get mad at these kids

I mean honestly
what did you expect?

These kids,
their dreams have been
steam-rolled and paved
left with only concrete frontiers
to explore and exploit

expected to die only to thrive
taking over like kudzu

Nomads with ripped up shoes
and messed up hair
pushing soles against pavements gray

through the industrial and commercial
wastelands of these cities

their hearts beating
like urethane wheels on sidewalk cracks

click-clack-click-clack, click-clack-click-clack

Skateboarding is not a crime
More importantly it's not a sport

If you have to call it anything
call it an art form
and like any other art form
it has the power to bring about change
turning parking lots into performance spaces
well-waxed ledged into altars of worship

Christian Hosoi pulled enough Christ-Airs
that he started to believe in Jesus
and I'm not sure about Jesus
but I believe in Christian Hosoi

The same way I believe in bombing
suburban hills at 2 o'clock in the morning
on 4 hours of sleep with caffeine
serving as a poor substitute for adrenaline
knees wobbly to match my wheels

I've found myself collecting scars like this
too many times before

# WHEN YOU TELL A BOY HE IS BEAUTIFUL

by Jason Bayani

The kids who used to beat me growing up never hit me
in the face. It's as if all I learned during those years
was how to hide the terrible things that were happening
between us. I know how dense the sound is of a knuckle
popping the fabric of my jacket sleeve. The sound dropped

me with it. My father used to rail on me
because I wouldn't walk upright, he said
you have to draw your shoulders back.
Like men do. I thought this would only leave
my heart exposed. And there is no place
for a boy who leaves these things open.

I know the exact place you can hit a person in the chest
to take the breath from them. You take the breath,
you take the heart. Because hearts are too loud in
all the wrong ways, and we only speak in low tones.

When you tell a boy he is beautiful, he will grow up
into a coil. When someone tells me that I am beautiful
my fingers ball into a fist. The first time I ever beat
another kid, I slammed his head to the ground
while I was crying for my mother. I'd like to say
that I am the most delicate person who has ever
punched someone in the face. But it's very easy to break

a boy and make him pretend he is not broken. I never fought
because I am the toughest person in the room. I've only
ever fought because I had nowhere else to put it. Sometimes
the worst way to live with violence is to not know how to live

without it. Maybe that is what a curse really is. That I would wish
something so terrible upon you as a cycle repeating.

I live in cities of men who have no regrets. Of men
who do not know the meaning of the word quit.

Who shake want and desire by the lapels until
it has something to offer them. I believe
that sometimes the world needs you to have a little
quit inside. That regret, keeps you honest.
And we don't get to deny who we hurt.

We always want too much anyway. We say
we want the world. But the world is too big,
and all it has to tell you is everything
you don't have. There's nothing more honest
than a quiet room. Nothing that will knock you
on your back more than knowing that nobody
has ever lied to you more than yourself.

When I was a kid they used to make me clean
the chalk boards. It was the quietest part of my day.
I'd be alone long enough I'd start playing with the muck
between my fingers. The dirt of me is the dirt of me.
I got an anger that puts the worry to my bones.

If I was truly honest I would say that love
is the thing I keep closer to my own chest.
That I wish I could know what it is like
to be touched without recoiling. That I could
tell someone they are beautiful or hear them
tell me the same without flinching.

# & MY MOTHER NOTICES SOMEONE ELSE'S BLOOD ON MY HANDS

by Danez Smith

'*Is it paint?*' she asked of the slender red
swirls making my knuckles pretty.
I managed a 'no,' hoping she wouldn't dig
into my hands' sudden & awful glamor.
Sunshine's blood on my fist (no I did
not uppercut sky, pull back a mess
of bright bones), I struck a light

skinned boy with big, chamomile eyes
who tried to steal my wallet out the new jeans
my mother said not to wear, but did
folded on the side of the crumbling court.
Oh, the soft music of cartilage collapsing
his face surrendering to the rule
of my ashy, small hand, blood stains my ring

finger, marries me to every cut on his face,
every purple, pregnant swell bloating his body.
'*What did you eat?*' I wanted to tell her
I ate a boy's pride covered in ranch & hot sauce
or I gobbled my own laugh, deep for the first time
while he fell to the ground, or I tenderized his lips
with these two black jackhammers I just discovered

or I ran, greedy for my own sweet life
when Sunshine went to tell his brothers
Smoot & Wop, high schoolers whose fists
begged for blood, not names. I knew my name
was not David. I didn't speak a word
to my mother, just walked past her, praying

she said nothing as I'm sure a man had done
to her before. I didn't go to the court
for two weeks. When I showed up, no one spoke
of my victory or cowardice, we just hooped.
That's all we wanted to be there for.

# ZELOPHOBIA - FEAR OF BEING JEALOUS

by Fatimah Asghar

*After Jamaal May*


In the sandbox I watched parents at the park
pick up their children,
twirl them around to a handholding car ride home,
while I walked, alone
under a freshly painted stain glass of a sky.

In the morning, when the clouds had the courage
to lantern again,
I made my own bagged lunches & wrote notes
I pulled out at the cafeteria table.
All the children traded their momma-made

sandwiches for my bag of candy. I would bite
into their breaded love,
dawn it around me like it was my own kitchen
chill my stomach into a fridge
& kept the memory of being full for hours.

Kids asked me why I wore hand-me-down stains
big as a tent, why I didn't know Gap or Nike,
why I sat alone reading during mother/father day
card-making.

When I speak of void, I speak of a hunger
a sandwich will not fill.
When I speak of empty I speak of the way a cave
will scream another voice
so as to not be amid its own lonely.

When I speak of silence, I speak of how everything
becomes a drunken tilt,
a slow shatter, the insides of your throat
a smelly spill across the floor.
How your legs vibrate with the wake of your empty.

When you are old enough to be put on display
people will call you a survivor.
Say you make a beautiful mosaic, congratulate you
on your broken. You will build
yourself into the hero of your every story.

Inside, everything will still be a slow shatter
screaming back your own alone.
But they, those who you have fooled
will hold you up,
a jagged prism of the glass you came from

lanterning the sky.

# SIMULACRUM

by Cristin O'Keefe Aptowicz

At the coffeehouse, I'm known as granola and yogurt.
At the supermarket, I'm known as large coffee, strong.
The old waiters in Queens called me *Christine*, because
I couldn't correct them after nine years of mistakes.

To the first boy I ever kissed, I'm probably the girl
with a last name he can't remember. To the second boy
I ever kissed, I am likely the brunette friend of the blonde
he really wanted to kiss. To my teachers, I was the front row,

the raised hand, the extra credit. To my poetry friends,
I am the deadline, the push on the shoulder. To my non-poetry
friends, I'm the poet. To my mom, I'm Cristin. To my dad,
I'm Pumpkin. To my nephews, I'm the person standing right

next to Uncle Shappy. I've answered to Professor Aptowicz,
to Ms. Cristin, to *Hey You!* I've been the new girl, the old
hand, the affable host. I've answered to a cleared throat,
to an awkward silence, to a snapped finger. This is all to say:

I wonder how you think of me now: am I still the crazy girl?
the loud one? the one who'd never go away? I know I was
the world's most transparent mystery, the persistent email,
the Christmas cookies you never wanted, hand-delivered.

If we met today, I hope I wouldn't be just an apology.
I hope I'd be the laugh in your fist, the second pancake,
the spilled coffee sipped from a saucer. I want to be that
great joke you accidentally forgot, the one that's still funny.

# STATUS

by Raymond Antrobus

When you find out your dad had a heart attack,
you wonder if you should update your Facebook.
You wonder if *one parent less* should be your status.

Maybe you change your profile picture,
upload one of you in your dad's arms as a white cotton baby,
where his face is a bright heart
                              smiling into your black newborn eyes.

People will *like* that.

It will make your relationship look like the kind you wanted,
          like he always knew how to hold you.

Like how he held
your handlebars on the bike you wanted
     that he bought
          and you wobbled
through London Fields and  he said
     peddle faster as he ran,
ran beside you, and you screamed
don't let go, don't let go

and he said you'll be fine and you wanted
to believe him and then he let go and you
rode, rode
and he threw proud arms in the air and bellowed
that's my boy, that's my boy!

But that's not what happened.

It's what was meant to have happened

# DRAGONS

by Rachel Jackson

*"Fairytales do not tell children that the dragons exist. Children already know that dragons exist. Fairytales tell the children that the dragons can be killed."- GK Chesterton*

We build bunk beds out of couches
stack cousins
on brothers
on nieces
Leather from the couch's seats
Forces
your cheek to be
smooth

It is a lullaby
massaging faces
and ears
drowning
out
stampedes of search parties
looking for your mother
under the nearest crack
rock

There is a vein on your ankle
puffing its chest out
for attention

We all have one

Dignity chopped up
with denial
snorted
throughout our lineage

royal blue hidden
entryways
that elevate our father's throne
even higher
parading the insides
of our elbows
during family reunions

No need for long sleeves
Admire
the crevices between our toes

Play games
with our family
High and seek
with track marks
hot potato
with relative's couches
that will force your cheek
smooth

We welcome cloaked addiction
It is the thread
that sews us together
without it
we'd be separated,
exposed to it
strung out

Monster
We already know
where you hide
Syringes give you neck cramps

Instead
Come
Spread your wings
over well groomed adults
And silent children
Littered with blisters
from mopping their mother's
face prints off the floor

Why do you need
your metal spoon so much?
This is family dinner time
Just need
forks and knives
and everyone's insides
to remain clean

White powders
and greasy thumbs
smear the edges of candid moments
Put up the photos over
decorations in the walls
shaped like
fists when coming down

Gaunt roots prohibit
communication
Dig deep in soil
and clutch
the sparse nutrients in fiction

Our stories
engraved in our bark

I'm sorry you believe us

We'll give you fairytales
about killing dragons
elaborative narratives
about bonding rehab trips

We be creative story tellers

Replaced
the abundance of
heroine in our blood
with
fantasy female heroes
fighting in the streams under our skin

Continue to welcome
the leather seats
of the communal couch

They will always
play bunk bed for our
cousins,
brothers
and nieces

They will always
shove
opiate-free
family gathering
fantasies
between your ears

They will always
force your cheeks
to remain careless,
oblivious
and smooth.

# YOU SOMEHOW STILL GUIDED ME TO SAFETY

by Katharen Hedges

I remember the last moments I ever shared with grandpa.
He was lying under white sheets,
like once pale paper consumed by flame: he was withering and gray.
When he died you said he left us nothing.
I used to think that was because he never had anything to give,
so I thought your death would be quite similar.

I sat in grandpa's hospital room and thought of you.
I imagined the dramatic death scenes
from all the movies I have watched with dead fathers.
At first attempting to cut and paste from them
the right frame of words to place around an impossible phrase.
But then I thought about how most movies lied.

There was no background music,
no piano to prepare me for what I was seeing.
There was no glowing aura of light surrounding his death.
It was ugly.
And the moment was ugly because my next impossible phrase:
the only three words that ever mattered, I failed to say.

I did not want my last words to grandpa to be a lie.
So I told him,
"I used to think I loved you, but that was before
I realized you can not love someone unless you know who they are."
I barely cried.
My tears walked the tightrope between falling and clinging
desperately to my waterline.
They did not want to feel the salty sting of shame as they ran down my
cheeks.

I did not plan for my last words to him to be a regret.

They say that pride is the most deadly sin and now I think I know why.
It is because what Mom told me was true.
She said I have a small child inside of me,
that I need to love her like she was my most precious gift.
I am beginning to learn who she is.

She does not fear the truth like I do.
I know that rejecting you completely,
scaring you away, would be way easier than watching you walk again,
than letting my heart feel satisfied and contented only for it to be taken.
I know the joy is not worth the pain anymore.
But she,

she would not be so selfish.
I do not know her very well but
there is one thing I know she would do
the only useful thing you ever told me to do.
She would love you in spite of yourself.
She would know that loving you was the best thing that she could do,
That fighting to love you was the only way to protect herself,
so she would not despise you for hurting her.

she would forgive you.
and I will fight to because
I do not want my next words to you to be a lie,
so my last words to you will not be a regret.
they will be silent
there will be your thick calloused hands
intertwined with my long tan fingers
there will be lungs inhaling heaven and exhaling Earth
there will be eyes admiring brown and gold irises
there will be memories of a little girl a top Daddy's knee
pretending to be driving

there will be the memory
of stars
of the soothing rattle of your semi-truck,
even though
the rain pounded violently against the wind shield
vision blinded
you somehow guided me to safety

# AND AS FOR THE MARROW

by Ronnie K. Stephens

I will call him Father, but not before he follows brother
to Viet Nam. Still small, he learns to fly quickly
and grounds himself in Amsterdam.

He never sees the war. Family tradition.
Still does not know the fury of bullets taking flight,
does not scrub the dead from his hands like demons.
But the drugs wind through his body like barbed wire
for ten more years. He is full of fences and he will leave you
bloody if you come calling for the boy he hung in the clouds.

He will call me Surprise with his first breath,
Son with his second. Chases higher pay through five jobs
in my first year. My mother grows weary of the turn around
after my second birthday. She works herself to stranger
in my eyes. He does not visit for three years.
Spends lifetimes on Clean before he returns
for the boy in the clouds, a bible still tight as stones
against his breast. He calls Savior in his sleep.

Mother sticks close to home. Works two jobs
when she has to, but never misses dinner at the table
or Dragnet on Saturday night. This is our routine.
One bedroom to two, apartment to house with backyard,
vacation at Grandma's to Disneyworld in the Spring.
She does not tire. Or does not show it. Father finds factory,
grinds Dependent into his bones. He will never miss
another summer, another holiday.

This is where I come from. This is me.
I am six shades of stubborn, a back wet with sweat
in the early parts of the day, hay bales hanging heavy
in a young man's hands, biscuits and gravy in the morning,
gospel songs in the kitchen. I wear Courage like a curse.
Still do not know the fury of bullets or the weight
of blood on the hands. I am buried in black dirt
on a hillside in Texas.

I am the son of single mother, fingers swollen
from clipping coupons, skillets full of hamburger
and leftover vegetables, six hours of sleep,
Saturday mornings at the soccer field.

Call me woman. I wear her like a medal,
like a past unbound and unflinching.

Call me blue collar. Call me sweat on the neck
and baths in the whiskey barrel out back.

I still pump water some days. Still feel the prick
of blackberries on the vine, the bruise of weed

in the bed. Still smell the slow burn
of a broke down Ford on the hill, the sweet pine
of early Autumn, biscuits and gravy on Sunday morning.

Call me what you will. I carry histories in my marrow
and I will not buckle. I never learned how.

# FALSE PROPHET

by Stevie Edwards

Dad says I'm the most miserable person he's ever met.
He is always saying this
as I stir the milk into my morning coffee,
pin back stray hairs, pace the living room asking my empty
apartment what I am missing
to begin my day. I try to imagine him painting
my pregnant mother's toes in sloppy sideways strokes
so she'd look down and smile over
her big belly. She says he did this.
On an early date he offered to pay
for the jacket she wanted in the mall window—
knee-length, red leather. She agreed
to him paying half.
He must have been tuck-tailed when he realized
he could never make her happy
sustainably. I can't blame him
for trying to decorate a long-dead tree:
needleless, her brittle branches always waiting
to catch fire. He is always saying
to get out of his house if I don't like it,
and I am always packing, always leaving,
hopping into a friend's car, a boyfriend's car,
anything that moves me
further from his words. I am trying to learn
new words (testaceous, affined, succor)
to speak reverently of the world
without him.

# HOPE CHEST

by Katie Wirsing

When the trees fell down
And the lights went out
An audible breath was held around the city
Soft as an infant's heartbeat
Heavy as a second chance

When the rain took a pause
And the lightening became not that bad
We rode our bikes free as the day we were born
Naked from the ground up
There has always been magic in a storm
even if the weatherman didn't see it coming

I am a storm the weatherman did not see coming.
I have developed my very own Twelve Step Program.
It's all about realizing yourself as a human being.
The first step is acknowledging that You Are
I am working on it constantly

The apologies I have yet to make in this life
are to the trees that fell the hardest going down
My spinal cord
Has never been great at weathering the storm
I am my very own fight and flight response system
I yell real loud while I run

But I have come around
More than once to this very same place in the forest
I have broken my own record off its turning track
Repeating to myself things I know to be true
There are ten thousand things I definitely should have told you

When I was fifteen my father sat me down at our kitchen table
with five shots of wild turkey lined up like
hey baby on the tongue of a teenage boy
in a suburban basement you knew better than.
It was less punishment than learning opportunity
But it took the better part of a crying hour to get them all down

To this day that is the most drunk I have ever been
But at fifteen it is difficult to appreciate
such awesome attempts at parenting
So out of spite I refused to allow myself to get sick
This is why I blame my father for the way I hold things in
Communication has never been the key to my broken hope chest

I blame my mother for my bleeding hope chest
That has nowhere to run
Some days I feel like a volcano with a plug stuck in my drain pipe
I am an excellent learner
Terrible at talking back

I have always found it easiest to hang my dirty laundry in a closet
With the door closed
And a padlock
I am not good at asking for help
I am not good at taking a stand

I am the kind of person who makes lists of things to tell my therapist
When I see my therapist I will list her this

One
There are mornings I wake up, already crying
Like the weight was too heavy
Even for my dreams

Two
Unworthy is a word that takes up so much space

Three
On the days that I believe in God
Life is easier
On the days I don't, I am nothing but a poison circling the drain

Four
Whatever unholy is
I have been that
Whatever holy is
I am dying to become


Five
I imagine when you decide you are enough
Peace is a feeling that finally makes sense

The last one I always say as a question
A hopeful song

# BAND GEEK.

by Rob Sturma

The tuba sits in the back of the band room,
brass fumble and elephant lung.
He knows his place is to be backbone to the melody.
He is the two and the four of the tempo, bass clef bashful
and just wanting to be part of the dance.

He looks at the back of a lot of heads
that rarely turn to listen to his harrumph and plod.
And there she is, rows in front of him,
the clarinet.   The stuff of sonatas, sleek,
smooth embouchre and trill.
He knows she isn't perfect; he's heard the squeaks
and breathiness from her section before.

And he sees her admiring the saxophone
when that guy begins to weave his way around the room
weaving jazz bop seduction songs.
There's always a saxophone that gets first look.
All collar up, Coltrane and Parker pedigree.

*Someday, he muses, someday I will meet her,*
*somewhere far away from these horrible uniforms*
*and John Philips Sousa parade marches.*   There
will be no sheet music then, no predetermined tempos.
They will not have their instruments in front of them
and although he still may have the confidence of a tuba player,
she will see something solid in him
that a million saxophones never wanted to provide.

Their conversation will become trills and low tones.
An awkward waltz with two unlikely players.
Someday she will weave melodies for him soft and perfect,
and he will do his level best to remain her backbone.

# 10 THINGS I WANT TO SAY TO A BLACK NERD

by Omar Holman

*after Jenifer Falu*

1
It's so hard being a black nerd

2
The books you love
don't have many heroes or villains that look like you
It's not the color but the content of
The characters that keep you reading

So writer Dwayne McDuffie,
helps build a diverse cast of heroes
so we could see our reflection as a mirror full of miracles

3
You thank God for Donald Glover and his songs as Childish
Gambinobecause you are down for community and these other
people are Glee fans.

Listening to him is the like having Nikola Tesla
sitting shotgun in The Delorean
while doing Pi ...sorry, "donuts"
in a Game Stop parking lot as Tesla says,
"Is that the new Neil deGrassse Tyson mixtape?
HOMIE, TURN. THAT. UP!"

4
Y-slope intercept is the algebraic form of any gangsta lean
and you crip walk to a different Pythagorean theorem

5
There is nothing on this Earth rarer than a black nerd girl
anytime you see proof that they exist it makes
you Dance Dance revolutions round your heart

If she has natural hair and wants to converse about con-verse?
+10 damage points,
Talks trash whenever she beats you in Mario Kart? +25 skill points
Cosplays, writes her own fan fiction, watches Adventure Time
or knows her way around MLA formatting?.... There's no calculation
for how sexy that is

6
When you get the girl, you'll remember every detail
like how the paint on her nails chips into isolated islands

When you get the boy, you'll reminisce
on how he made oblivious look like the new abstinence

When you have each other,
you'll recall the memory as an 8-bit adventure;
call it old-school, call it classic, whatever symbolizes
that the moment was an arcade high score you achieved together

7
Your most hood moment was when
they killed Ned Stark on Game of Thrones
even as I mention it now, inside you're reenacting Larry's
youtube video saying,

"They killed my Dude Ned Man"
Lyin Lannsiters did him dirty son

To those of you that don't know
For nerds Ned Stark's death is equivalent to
When Hip-Hop heads lost Biggie Smalls

8
Your black friends say hand over your black card
because you never watched "The Wire",
Your white friends think having watched "The Wire"
it's okay for them to say they're "blacker" than you are

Yet you're the first one they'll come to
when there is a new super hero movie out...

"Everybody wanna be a [nerd] but don't nobody wanna be a [nerd]"

9
A nerd off is the closest you will ever come to battle rapping
It occurs when anyone corrects you on a topic obnoxiously

If you engage in this Battle Royale of facts
Your retort should always sound something like this,
"Actually, "Hear me roar" are the words of House Lannister
not "A Lannister always pays his debt"...

and once you see that look of "Oh he bout murder me" on their face
You Highlander them with a stare that's says,
"You goin get this work, cause I'm a Grey Skull graduate
with a Masters in the Universe and you ain't bout this life b"

10
It is so hard being a black nerd
Slinging six sided di on the block
Keeping it retro when you pop out
the Nintendo 64 like it's a six-fo impala

All black everything
Because that's what you've always been...everything.
From chuck taylors to lightsabers
From "Press Start" to "Game Over"

# OUR LORD JEEZLE PETE

by Shappy Seasholtz

My dad never cursed
At least not while us kids were around
And even when we weren't I'm not so sure he used the crude language
He had to endure everyday at the GM plant
Maybe he had enough of it at work and didn't want to bring it home
For his boys to pick up like a broken bottle
That would cause their mouths to bleed

Dad refused to take the Lord's name in vain
He was the President of the Congregation at Good Shepard Lutheran
Church
So he'd say "Jeezle Pete!" instead.
It confused Cristin when she first heard my dad use it in a sentence
And then she gave her heart to Jeeezle Pete
And walks down his path

My dad refused to let his emotions get the best of him
Even in traffic jams
Once we sat in Christmas shopping gridlock outside
of the Dayton Mall
"God bless their hearts!", he'd say looking at the long string of vehicles
ahead of us
"They just can't seem to get anywhere! Jeezle Pete!"

"Yes, John!" my mom snapped, "Bless their hearts for waiting til the last
minute to shop!"
Mom had not accepted Jeezle Pete into her heart quite yet.

So the next time life has got you
Waiting in line
Stuck in traffic

In any unpleasant situation
Just take a deep breath
And sing the praises of
Jeezle Pete
Our patient Lord.

# HOW THE GOOD SOUTHERN GIRL WENT AWOL

by Molly Meacham

She packed her lipstick first.
All five shiny tubes
pale pink to cinnamon stick
bullets to be loaded,
soldiers at attention.

She plucked ma'am and sir
from behind teeth.
Made her mouth a harmonica.

She broke ranks,
watched feet.
She learned that meeting eyes
means finding landmines or loose soil
in her path.

She opened her grandmother's cookbook
to fruit tea, cheese grits,
and duct taped the ingredients to her chest.

She lifted the family Bible, tore out
the 23rd Psalm, swallowed it.
Left the rest.

She slipped off her cross, kicked it
between the teeth of her pillows
for her parents—an identification
of holy, but

until she was safe
past the gravel driveway,
she did not march in her shoes.

# ON BREATHING

by Jade Sylvan


When you learn that most of what you've read and studied for in school
is a crude approximation or shrewd merchandizing tool

and your lungs will one day shrivel, and your heart will fizzle out
when tricks of science peter, and religion's sick with doubt

and your rapist's hands weren't dirty, and forgiveness won't clean deeds
and just cause something's dirty doesn't mean it seeds disease

and your safety net's dispassion on this centripetal whirlwind
and without the lights and makeup movie stars look like your
girlfriend

and your doctor's a mechanic, and your therapist's a nut
and your head and heart betray you till you only trust your gut

and Hitler was a vegan, and an artist, and a Jew
and Hussein was not a devil, and your father's half of you,

it can be hard to keep on going, but you do.

When knees wake stiff, reminding you that death's your only
birthright
and there seems to be some script you lost to move across the
earth right

and soil swallows all your clothes, books, houses, clocks, and letters
and credit scores and income are the first things in the shredder

and your synapses are labyrinths that coax desirous heat
and beneath their skins your enemies, like you, are only meat

and the pattern of his birthmarks and the odd bend of his hand
are death when you recall them, and Inferno when you can't

and the upright slouch in alleyways while Rupert Murdoch thrives
and money is a symbol, and your children won't survive

and vodka seems to work as well as any cheerful pill
and college girls and soldiers look so young, and younger still,

it can be hard to keep on moving, but you will.

When masturbation's better than most lovers' hunger pangs
and love produces chemicals, like chocolate and teen angst

and you only feel by bleeding, and Top Tens have made love cheesy
and all your pain's cliché, but that still doesn't make it easy

and once you struck a song while wrestling with an old piano
and played it to an empty hall and hummed the sad soprano

and the moon will never care for you, the sun will make you blind
and there're rooms locked in your body even you will never find

and her back is pressed against your chest, her scapula are wings
and sex is high and sacred, just like every other thing

and your belly's slightly fat and gapped with stretch marks where it grew
and you know you'll never meet someone who'll love you more
than you

and you wake up in some room alone, the sunlight cold as flan
your skin saran against the dawn, the door, a businessman,

it can be hard keep on breathing, but you can.

# CAPRICE IN ELEMENTARY

by Aaron Samuels

Darlene said you were gay,
if you stepped on the purple tiles.
This is true.

I used to jump for this girl, followed her
around the edge of the cafeteria,
never stepping on the purple tiles.

I used to wait for winter to end.

One time an albino boy named Stacy
stepped on purple.
He was a gay boy

gay gay gay gay gay gay gay.
I used to stand still in turtlenecks and watch
But really I used to hide

under orange leaves with my mouth shut
and Stacy used to say so *what if I am!*
And then his nose used to be broken

and leaves used to be stuck
to his body with dried blood and I used
to be skinny and have small hands

and tuck my turtlenecks into dungarees
when the mornings were purple and orange.
The schoolyard was never big enough

so I pulled a skull cap over my black
curls, tied my waist with a braided belt.
I used to be orange tiles in the hallways,

and Stacy used to walk on purple
and be covered in it and I tell his story
and pretend that I used to be Stacy,

used to have iron pipes in my arms,
that I used to walk home every day
with a face covered in brown scabs,

that the New England wind used to remind me
how many entrances there were into my skin,
that I was not a small burrowing creature,

that I was more than a boy who just stood
and watched, more than a pile of leaves
in an Edgewood schoolyard,

that I used to survive the winter.

# DELHI'S BELLY

by Carrie Rudzinski


Prabakar tells me India
is accustomed to Western clothing,
rocks his head side to side,
"You'll be fine, Carrie."

New Delhi's belly
is wrapped in curdled violet,
the smog so thick
we could swallow
a dust storm for breakfast;
The India Gate a cloud resting
just across the shoulder of traffic.
My brother is a blur;
too excited, too smothered, too eager
and dashing, his camera a dagger.
I am a stone tossed
at the side of the road, breathless,
the heat at my back.

Two men begin to cross the street –
howling – their eyes are bowls
I have licked clean dozens of times.
One is holding a handful of balloons;
an ice cream cone of protests
his tongue would devour whole.
Calloused hands clutching
for a Messiah. My body is a coil,
a trail of smoke rising.

Too quickly the man
who has been our guide all day,
the man who has spent
too much of our money,
the man who dresses
like he is going to a nightclub
ten years too late,
his baseball cap
married to an American name,
steps between me and the world:
a sudden curtain.
A bear trap.
I am no longer just a white woman
in knee length cut offs
and a shaved head.

I am a woman
standing with a man.

Later, Javits would laugh,
tell me that Western clothing
"brings out the devil in men."
That if I were sexually assaulted
in public, I had asked for it.

I tell him, surprise is a funny word.
I tell him, I am a woman.
It does not matter the country I am in.
It does not matter the clothing that I wear.
The world is still a beast
and he is always hungry.

# BIG BAD WOLF

by Katelyn Lucas


If the big bad wolf had told the story

He would have discussed the length
of little red riding hood's skirt

How she really shouldn't have been alone out there
in the woods so late

How that dinner in her basket smelled so good
and how he just couldn't help himself.

He would have spoken of his own teeth,
how they were only ever not enough.

We would all sit back and say,
"What interesting grief you have!"

and he would reply,
"...the better to fool you with, my darlings
the better to fool you."

# A PERIOD PIECE

by Jamila Woods


Someone has painted the Sistine Chapel
red.  The ceiling is dripping
dripping down the walls—

Wet paint! Do not touch! Wet paint here!

Do not put your hands there
unless you're fond of finger-painting
(sacred.) Flowers and stick figures
all look alive when drawn with this hue.

Why do you make that face
when I tell you about the masterpieces
I release from my skin?
It's not every day you shed
a Miró or Rothko from your gut.

Today, a young girl found a palette
in her panties and feared for her life.
Tomorrow, she will learn to waddle
with the weight of polyethylene coated
cotton between her legs.

Her mother will smile bleary eyed, show her
the cabinet beneath the bathroom sink
with the pretty yellow, green, pink, purple
plastics. She'll tell her to choose a canvas
to catch the leakings of the mural
from her ceiling.

(Don't ever let it feel like a secret.
Remember that it is not a curse.)

Next month, she will learn to let the cloth
bubble, toil, trouble for thirty seconds
before rinsing with hot water. She will learn
to let the corners of her eyes burn, but not bubble
over when the boy points and laughs at the cherry
circle blooming at the back of her pants at lunchtime.

(Don't ever let it be called mess.
Always look the sales clerk in the eyes.)

There was a time when women were encouraged
to place their money in a box, avoid speaking
to drugstore salesmen, and quietly take the bag
of sanitary napkins from the counter themselves.

Grass, rabbit skins, sponges, knit fabric, wet soil—
So many buckets set out to catch this peculiar rain
we make. These waste bins filled with bushels of
molten ruby wrapped in tissue could have been
a multitude of angels in my womb. They could have been
a freshly painted apartment for some new tenant not yet come.

(Don't ever let it feel like a burden.)

Even when you are sprawled sweaty across the bedspread,
light headed, doped up on Motrin, clutching your abdomen
asking: Where did this strange thundering appendage
come from? Who took my organs out and left this churning
chunk of matter in its place?

(It may never make you feel pretty.
It will make you feel alive.)

Tonight, mother will find wet splotched garments hung up
on the shower rod, her daughter cowering near the bathroom
sink trying to remember when, where, how she could have
possibly made this big of a mistake.

Mother will find towels and brown bottles,
give them to her daughter, tell her:

> Priceless exhibits
> stream down your legs.
> You are a museum
> unto yourself.

# REAL ESTATE

by Jesse Welch


If you name me home
I will not deny you
I will be floor and walls
Windows and doors
I will be faded couch
Mismatched drapes
The Super Nintendo
You got for your 3rd birthday
I will be drafty

I will be flickering light bulb
The hole in the wall
No one mentions
I will be burn marks in the recliner
Deep stains
Cabinets slammed off their hinges

If you are to live here
Know
I am no model home
I am a weather-worn project
You will never afford to repair
A place to keep your secrets
With closets you should not open

# THE BEES

by Asia Calcagno

He said *when the bees die*
*we all go. Tiny Gods*
he called them
while we sat that summer
at Cherry Orchard Farms.

We were allowed to buy
souvenirs. I got apple butter
my brother, cider, my father,
a jar of honey with a slab
of comb inside.

I waited months until the container
was empty to finally touch the comb.
When the time came, I bent, bit
and chewed until my mouth foamed.
It was waxy, like crayon. Tasteless.

Once, neighborhood kids threw stones
at the tree in our front yard.
Petite hands aimed high. Rocks beat
on the outside of a vibrant, buzzing cove.
Each struck a heartbeat. It shook.

The sound, a malfunctioning machine.
My father watched from the window.
The fire department took smoke to it.
He was quiet then. A silence filled with fog.
He cursed the children and what they did

to the Gods. The next day,
while running barefoot at the park I got stung.
I felt guilty when the venom entered.
I wiped the dot of brains and guts
from the bottom of my foot. I smeared
the innards onto the grass and search for holiness

if there were any at all.          Ten years later,
I wake in an apartment teeming with bees.
My lover doesn't want us
to die this way. I take a heavy boot
and crush each one

against the window, and then the wall
and the bathroom sink.
After I murder the last one
the apartment becomes quiet.
For a long time, I wait for the sound.

# HAIKU

by Marc Smith


Fools fly from blossom
To blossom seeking to find
Only themselves sweetened.

A friend's heart speaks love
Questioning the path taken.
Agreement binds us.

In darkness find light.
In chaos order to chaos.
In love an answer.

Insidious bed
Cloaking ambition in doubt
Soooooo warmmmmmm ......... Get UP! LIVE!

We break things trying
To be unbreakable. Flower
Stems bend with the wind.

# NEXT LIFE SOUNDTRACK

by Buddy Wakefield


Having pumped panic buttons and pedal metal down the throats of
freeways
and crashed like heavy glass ashtrays into our own homes
broadside
with department store force and a gas can,
distended stomachs and God's holes...
Having shown off our momentum for yawning
as a clever way to denigrate deeds of kindness...
Having created enough minimum wage faith
to distract orphans from the exit rows
then thrown holding pattern parties in their honor
only to present each other with our own names on gold plaques bolted
to a fountain of toll booths used to dressed up up in our go go
go and gone uninterrupted
by the signs that serve to encourage calming down,
it is good to know I have at least been loosening my grip on the
expectation
that our thumbs will necessarily oppose each other
in the next life.


There is a next life
and it is my understanding we will not necessarily
be binge-drinking bros
wearing Greek lamp shades paying for friendships
based on how pornographic our breath smells.
I will not necessarily find myself rationalizing with computer
gamers
and overly polite customer service robots
about how much life is lost on alternative realities
or how much violence peaceful consumers cause.
The results of our language cannot be programmed.
There is no proper way to hide the rampage with whom we have been
banking.

There are no words thick enough to conceal the transparencies
in these stories we have crafted
out of loopholes and nothin' but net.

The next life is being offered to us daily
via live streaming satellite by entitled white rabbits and tragedy addicts
dragging their
fingernail
file
cabinets
across records of the damage my nerves have done.
You inglorious preachers of a sensational game.
Sensations and games are at the root of why we are walking so
inefficiently,
warped 45's with credit card swagger charging up a sad sad path
like Ray Charles singing Seven Spanish Angels
to the bottom of the barrel
in
broad daylight. Stop congregating in the valley just because an echo
sounds good when it agrees with itself.
A trajectory of misery – at this point – seems intentional.
We have all the information we need to see clearly.
We are no longer unaware toddlers on the landscape of consciousness.
It is no longer cute to crap ourselves.

Get the sticky off your buns and roll with me.
Brush the hair from your eyes and comb over.
Stop paying the dentist for a night guard if it's still allowing your jaw to
pulverize the truth.
The truth is: You feel fine, right now.
We are a point of complete, not a soundtrack to the next life.
The future
gets no say in who we are.
Settle your debt and logout.
Thank you
for laughing at the joke several lines ago about sticky buns.

That was sweet. This is nuts.
Listen…

Having listened
to the parentheses of passive aggression
and made far too much bracket in response,
incriminating ourselves as sucker punches and suckerfish, soaker hoses
and preying on the dead weight
of fashion-forward food for overpopulation,
having inflicted the most amount of pleasure with the least harm done
then called it progress,
I am still, without fail, eligible to remind us that there is a reason
the future gets so agitated by our advances.
We are not built to barge ahead of ourselves in false fast-forward on a
flat fifth wheel made out of spokespeople for progress
who fly off the handle whenever anyone taps the breaks.
Throw it in park.

Gauge the pressure.
Renunciation is not a frigid concept.
It is okay to abandon the tackle practice
of having and crashing and having and crashing
through this circuit board of carrier pigeons carrying torch carriers
over an orchestra of strung-out sixteenth notes
composed with a matchstick that struck out and broke off but did not
burn up.
If the next life keeps finding us in these uncomfortable positions
they might mistake us for honest.
How honest is it that we drink until we are dehydrated?
If my throat turns into carbonated leather

and you hang me like a lucky foot from the rearview mirror while
barreling down the freeway, toll booth after toll booth, in a heavyglass
ash tray, wondering how the hell freeways got so expensive, remember
this:

The White Rabbit is said to be a symbol of human beings who are pompous and belittling toward anything they deem less valuable than themselves, yet they grovel to accommodate anyone from whom they stand to gain.

To what end are you gaining?
I'm not speaking to our governments,
I'm speaking to the way we govern ourselves.
Make your stopwatch live up to its name.
We are not late for an important date,
we have simply shown up too early for the next life and forgot to knock,
forgot that the future doesn't want us to arrive.
It knows that if we do, it dies.
As if people on stilts really need you to offer them more gravity.

# WHAT'S IMPORTANT
by Marty McConnell

*for Caroline, and for me*


is to know that you will one day be happy
again. Happier than you were

with her, happier than has ever been possible. Focus
on what makes you

happy: a hot teacup against your belly. Fresh sheets.
Turning up the heat

in the apartment and cleaning naked as if it is August
and everyone you love

is coming over for breakfast. You have had love, and that means
your sternum is a divining rod

for both passion and grief. Because the tongue is the body's
strongest muscle, make it say

joy. Make it say *I am a factory of splendid things.* Make it say
*the octopus is the smartest animal*

*in the animal kingdom, and I am an octopus.* I am an octopus.
I am happy. The car that could

have ended me didn't. The lies that could have brined my insides
to bitterness, didn't.

Our survival was not an accident. Word on the street is,
you have muscles other

than the tongue. Take them for a walk
in the sun. Or, if it is April

in Chicago and therefore as grey as your actual hair,
in the rain. There are people

everywhere. Some of them are happy. You are one of them. I
am one of them. And it's

OK. You can be happy and have a baby. You can be happy
and create disconcerting images

of traditional Christian figures in compromising positions
using masticated fireflies

as paint. Someday somebody will love you for this.
or in spite of it.


Either way, you're an octopus. I'm an octopus. Say it:
*We are happy.* Say: *It's not so bad.*

# QUESTIONING INTENTION

by Bonafide Rojas

if the day presented a gift to you,
would you be prepared to accept it?
if the night allowed you to sleep,
would you thank her for it?
if time gave you the hours you seek for,
would you use them wisely?
when the truth comes to you,
do you reject it because it shows you're in the wrong?
in a conversation/debate/argument,
do you want to be heard or be right?
if people give you advice,
do you tell them you knew that already?
when someone asks you a question,
do you avoid answering by telling a story?
when you're upset,
do you try to make the other person feel bad?
when loving someone hurts more than anything,
do you not let go of pain because you're stubborn?
does revenge & spitefulness stay in your
system longer than the love did?
understand the road & its many intersections,
we never walk alone
there are guides that show us new vantage points,
be grateful people even want to help when someone says i love
   you,
what do you honestly feel?
why would you not believe them?
would you not believe what you respond with?

# HYPOTHETICAL NO. 1

by Annelyse Gelman

What if eyes were like teeth
so that around puberty your baby eyes would loosen and fall out
– you'd place them beneath
your pillow and wake damp between your legs with a silver dollar
under your tongue – displaced
by the grownup eyes buried all along in your eye sockets, like tulip
bulbs, only grownup eyes
were duller (there are no second chances, even in fantasy, especially in
fantasy) and more diffused
than baby eyes, so you squandered your adolescence lamenting
your mutilated vision
finally opting for the surgery that could restore your baby eyesight
even knowing the risk
you might be left utterly blind, having decided it would be better
to see nothing than to see
everything but the brilliance you once
took for granted
(as you came to me with flowers on your tongue
to see how many colors I could taste) – what would you do with me
then, with my factory
of regrets and my stupid objects, obstinately remaining what they are?

# HOME GARDENING MADE EASY

by Robbie Q Telfer


Did you know
that if you stick a pebble
into the ground that —
depending on the magic —
the pebble will grow into a giant
green slo-mo explosion?
Like a verdant lightning bolt
you flash-freeze?

Did you know that you can learn
the secret art of pebble-
whispering and make a mine-
field of nutrition, a firework
display of flavor, you can become
a mage-general of sunlight-
earth conversation, a wizard-
technician photographer making
3D snapshots of delicious
weedy dirt sneezes?

Gardener, guard-man, gourd-mongrel,
did you know you can sweep
the knowledge of millions of years
of human evolution into an idea
pile and you can tease the word
bubbles of millions of years of
plant evolution from moist flat
planet crumbles, from the piles
of millions of kinds of brown, you,
gardener lady, can ask the right
questions and get fistfuls of answers

in your stomach, with the right kind
of patience, the right kind of forgiveness?

Did you know there is a GPS
programmed into your chlorophyll
palms, there is a place where answers
are true and full of riboflavin, all the
seed pebbles are stacked in a perfect
pyramid in your brain, in a memory
you haven't yet experienced?

Did you know there are hundreds of different names for just tomatoes?

Here is an alphabetical list of some of my favorites:

Arkansas Traveler
Aunt Ruby's German Green
Banana Legs
Beauty Blanc
Black Brandywine
Black Plum
Black Seaman!
Blondkopchen
Bloody Butcher
Campbell's 1327
Caspian Pink
Cherokee Purple
Dingwall Scotty
Earl of Edgecomb
Eva's Purple Ball
German Johnson
Giant Belgium
Golden Treasure
Green Zebra
Halfmoon China

Hank!
Hartman's Yellow Gooseberry
Indigo Rose
Kentucky Beefsteak
Livingston's Perfection
Misouri Pink Love Apple
Mr. Stripey
Mule Team
Nebraska Wedding
Omar's Lebanese
Orange Oxheart
Peacevine Cherry
Prize of the Trials
Purple Calabash
Siberia
Snow White
Stump of the World
Tiny Tim
Yellow Perfection
Zapotec Pleated

Woman,
did you know we planted way
too many tomatoes?

Woman, did you notice
we're in the middle of this
field of tomatoes and I can't
see anything else except you
and these millions of dangling
hearts, like millions of juicy
shiny, sun-warmed hearts,
seed-filled hearts with billions
of tomorrow's hearts asleep
in the heart-seed-memory

of the tomato's hearts, we
are in a thump meadow of
remember and potential, did
you notice that? We'll have to
can this love, sun-dry this love,
bring baskets of it over to my
folks, and the internet said
it's okay for the dog to eat too.

Lady-friend, did you know
each morning is Spring, each
grow is feel, each field is us.
There is a sprout on my
uvula, there is my joycare
on a root, there is a map
of green surprises we're
cartographizing, did you know
we have a buttload of dirt
to whisperkiss together?

Oh you knew all that?
Ok. Just checking.

# BEAUTY

by André Schürmann


my conception of beauty is non-existent.

but I see it
when i hear it
when i read it
i can smell it
when i touch it
when i taste it

all senses in a spin,
a defense-cracking blend
an intriguing extract
the word-brew slowly thrown in
by nose or mouth or syringe
to blow your brain
and spread in you.

how to convey words in an attainable way?
how to be ready to receive?
rearrange syllables and let them play?
sway uncommon thoughts
in the melody, the rhythm, the array?
let poetry say.

its soul confuses so
it brightens, it dampens, it enlightens
sometimes it opens
forgotten space, maybe lost
poetry proves there is no god
we have to dread
its beauty gives us bread.

poetry cracks shells, breaks spells
invades mind, inundates heart
opens wombs and closes rhymes.
poetry is everything
that lingers between the lines.

fill these interspaces with your sorrow, your ecstasy
abound and overflow,
mould your hunger for the other
pour it into poetry
its language is for all

it fires at disparity, falsity, hypocrisy,
all foul forms.
poetry is a free body
in a place where everything and nothing rule.

poetry is sister, poetry is brother
poetry is always me and another
poetry is alive, it's alive
poetry gives, it hurts,
it takes
and makes ...

... a monster we have to feed
with the flesh of sound and feeling
that lead us through
to our healing.

a poem may cling
when we're gone
to console
the remaining.

# HORROR STORIES

by Benjamin Clark and Colin Winnette


You were a werewolf and I was a witch and we were on TV.
The show was about monsters coming to terms with modern life.
In the first episode you struggled to use a silent blender
and I tried to order a pizza online. In one of the best episodes
they filmed us in the bathtub. There were vampires in the background
leaning close and whispering to one another, shading their eyes
from all the artificial lights. A mummy curled outside the door
was mumbling in his sleep. We didn't know them
but we agreed they were good guys. It was part of the show.
We stuck it out in the tub when the others got bored, and took turns
pouring water over one another's shoulders from a small red bucket.

We were in an old apartment and the heating system clanged all winter.
I hear those are the episodes people tend to skip. The winter months.
Wrapped in blankets you can hardly tell we're monsters. We knew
the arc of the show, that you would inevitably eat me.
They wrote the last episode first and worked their way back.
I secretly set out to write a list of reasons why you shouldn't eat me.
I watched the old tapes, the early episodes, and it's all really incredible,
but it's hard to say how many viewers will hang on until the end.
Those that do will, on some level, know exactly what they're in for.
Like every time I've placed you in the tub,
and chained your wrist to that fragile pipe.

# THE STREET AFTER DARK

by Karen Finneyfrock

We left our cob-webbed kitchens
to float the lantern sidewalks—cursed goblin
children, hexed into witches and quarterbacks.

Past the questionable safety of our porches, we swam
to the buoy of the lamplight. The street's face was painted.
Trees pretended they weren't following us. Full moons
    squeezed
into the open mouths of pumpkins.

Some houses had doorbells, and some had knockers,
and fathers grinning vampire teeth. One mother offered
a bowl full of apples. From the bottom of her dress hung a tail.

Toilet paper dripped from hedges like white weeping
willows, styrofoam tombstones grew weedy in the lawns.
The night stepped closer when we weren't looking. We heard it
breathing before we knew it was there. The street tilted and turned
into rubber, and even the cowboys ran home.

We brushed our blacked-out teeth white again, while mothers
searched buckets for traps, taking ripped plastic wrappers,
and caramel apples,holding sugar tubes up to the light. They
looked for things we didn't know names for, waiting
in the bottom of the candy bag, disguised to our eyes as sweet.

# HOOKED CROSS

by Jesse Parent


Little brother,
look what they've done to me.

For millennia
I have woven myself into humanity's dreams,
raced comet-like across their collective consciousness.
As basic as a circle,
a hooked cross.
A child of lines and busy hands.
Simple. Recognizable.
They called me Swastika.

I was everywhere,
even in the one place I wished I wasn't.

I admit I was jealous of you, little brother
and the star you rose up on.
For I was just a hooked cross,
glossed over on cracked clay pots and deerskin teepees.
Hidden along with kisses on the collars of Chinese children,
ironically, to protect them from evil spirits.
All of Asia blended me into their backgrounds,
Jainism, Buddhism, Hinduism.
I could tell you where any temple was.
A sun symbol. A heart's seal. Eternity.
A minor celebrity on one continent,
a child's absent doodle on the rest.

He took me West, little brother,
told me to point right and lean,
hold the pose.

Shone a bright, white spotlight on me
while I danced on a red carpet.
They all waved at me, little brother.
I got caught up in the rush to become a major celebrity.
It was too late to turn back.
They slaughtered each other under my hooked shadow.
The smoke of their flesh darkening my form.
I let them make me into something horrible.
Simple. Recognizable. Detestable.

Humanity's dreams no longer idly trace my form
in innocent doodles.
Countless millennia may never wash away
the stench on my lines
no matter which way I turn.
A minor celebrity on one continent,
a symbol of hatred on the rest.
So many killed while I waved over them,
their murderers justifying themselves
by the meaning they put into my shape.
They killed for me.

You don't have my hooks, little brother,
but we have the same parents,
the same simplicity of lines.
We have had different men who have defined us
even if we have both been worn by popes.

My body count is well over 6 million, little brother.
Pray they do not start counting up the ones
that were killed for you.

# IT'S RISKY TO LOVE IN THE SEASON OF HUNTERS

by Desiree Bailey

*for Renisha McBride, Travyon Martin and the rest of us*

I.

And when the dark tightens around my neck
I think of vultures casting a shadow
just before the flesh breaks,
of the omen of crows nailed into the sky,
of gaping earth home
for black girl, for black boy

think my brothers, my lover
will writhe into horned creatures
to be gunned down
or strung up

that they walk with the promise
of carrion splayed
for the flies.

And when the dark trickles down my throat
I know that home is but a fading horizon
that here, I will always be out of body
I will always fall outside the lines,
that if I dare go missing, my name
will crawl beyond the reach of memory

that I am only a problem, a pest,
a damned spot, a gamebird, a bullseye, a neck
for a hook, a haunted, hunted thing.

II.

When I heard the news of the Zimmerman verdict, my body
collapsed into itself. Becky picked my lungs up off the floor.
Said I would need them for dancing. What I needed was to be
home in my neighborhood of foreigners with our chimera
accents. I needed the coffin silence of the Q85 bus cruising
down Merrick Blvd, the secret mourning of women behind
the frayed curtains of their weaves, the churn of the engine
emitting all our trapped sounds.


III.

Who are these friends who
smile
laugh   cry
twerk
praise Wu Tang
snap fingers
ask if our hair is real
study
walk arm in arm
are family
break bread
share crop t-shirts
and ice cream
go to the mall
go to the river
with us?

Who are they really
if they do not lament our dead?

# GANGSTA POETICS

by José Olivarez


I leapt off the top of the Sear's tower
Dared gravity to pull me down
That sucka tried to test me
But I just shook my head
Landed on my feet
Brushed the dirt and gravity off my shoulders
Took a step back towards the Sears Tower
And I was flying

     I'm gangsta

I was racing across the Universe at the speed of
Now
Ran into a star that was cramping my
Style
Blocking my attempts to pass
So I
Jumped from my planet onto that star
Landed on a cloud
Rode it to the ground
Left a crater the size of half a moon
Kicked up a mushroom cloud of dust
Then poured salt in the wound

     I'm gangsta

I scared twenty volcanoes into sinking underwater
When I sucked the lava out of a volcano,
Used it as mouthwash
Spat it back at the volcano
Twenty times hotter
Burned it into an ant hill

I'm gangsta

I'm gangsta
So watch your back
I've tortured
Death into touching himself
Laughing as he writhed in pain
Stay away
Because I'm gangsta
I threatened to drown time
In a pool of burning tar
And now clocks move on my command
Like
Tic
Toc
Never before

I'm gangsta

The sun once challenged my gangsta
Claimed it was more gangsta than me
Because the planets revolved around it
I slapped all of his rotating body guard
Now they orbit in elliptical patterns
Landed on Earth
Stared directly at the Sun
And it exploded in a burst of bright flames
Burned badly by my blazing stare

It hasn't challenged my gangsta since

If you looked up gangsta in the dictionary
I would reach through the pages
Rip your tongue out

And hang you with it
For even doubting whether or not my picture would be there
I'm the epitome of gangsta
Taught Mohammed Ali how to throw a punch
Grew tired of living in the dark
So I clapped
And all the stars lit up

     I'm gangsta

And if you ever cross the line between
"Keeping it real"
And
Fantasy
You too can be anything you want.

# GONE PING PONG
# (A GHAZAL FOR AN MC)

by Chancelier "Xero" Skidmore

Blood brother lyrical hustlers, we were halves that started pieces
Since seventh grade we word-played and spoke in ordered pieces

You and I led ciphers that leveled much better fighters
OTB and Seymourville reciters, we slaughtered pieces

Dropped out and graduated to blue collar servitude
Still servin' dudes and seekin' profits in larger pieces

Loquacious with the ladies, too crazy to not make babies
We stuck around to raise'em, and found time to father pieces

My phony matrimony came and went like Johns
Cooler than the Fonz was our bond for harder pieces

You shacked up then had to act up, break up and back up
Pick up and pack up, so many women watered pieces

Tears don't lubricate tongues, they only get hearts hung
When ours swung, luckily the daughters taught us pieces

When you lost your oldest siblin', we both kept scribblin'
I was buildin' in the lab with you when you recorded "Pieces"

I stepped away from rappin', more poetry fans were clappin'
You respected my passion's passin' like martyred pieces

You the producer, who'da thought that you would propose
A good woman pried open your nose, you snorted pieces

I long for when the local throng nagged us for our next song
Now I only learn about you through Sean with smarter pieces

We straighter than creases, but these hearts wear leashes
We both hold the handles, giving slack for broader pieces

When we wrote, our minds moved each other like telekinesis,
When we spoke, we finished a friend's phrases, shorter pieces

"Xero, I'm off to New Orleans, let's keep talkin' and ballin'"
I'm deflated cause we stopped yes-yallin', departed pieces

# DEATH FROM BELOW

by Tim Stafford and Dan "Sully" Sullivan

He told me I'm not allowed to get angry
because I'm white
I'm a male
and I'm straight

but he overlooked the fact that I'm
very
very
SHORT!

I mean I'm only five-foot-five
and even that's a lie
I'm only five-foot-four
Don't know what I was lying for
it must be my insecurities
my little man complex
The same things that make me try
to get muscles to flex
but they only go out
and not up

And high school?
high school was hell for me man
I had to overcompensate with a big mouth
and a quick wit

And everybody thought they were so funny
Everybody thought they were the first person to call me
shorty
shrimp
midget

oompa loompa
lollipop kid
Tiny Tim!

I've heard them all

I've heard them all

I have heard them all

So now
We're calling upon all our short people
our little people
our below the average height
of five-foot-eight PEOPLE!
Denied access to the roller coaster
because they don't make the minimum
height requirement PEOPLE!

Can't touch the rim PEOPLE!
Can't date girls in heels PEOPLE!
Can't reach the top shelf PEOPLE!

Our High fives
are really low fives PEOPLE!

Always having to give up the front seat
to those gangly, long, legged,
freak show, jolly green giant,
Too-Tall Jones, skyscraping PEOPLE!

Let's strap on some stilts
hide them under trench-coats
and together we'll penetrate the
tall man's headquarters

blending in with talk of basketball
and when the time is right
we'll cast off our coats and strike
with kicks to the shins
and uppercuts to the guts
holding the giants for ransom

Demanding they change the image of the ideal man
from tall, dark, and handsome
to short
pale
and we can still be handsome!

We want the ten percent pay
you been denying us
because now we know you've been lying

The short stacks of the world are now UNITED!
So look out Tally McTallface
Here's the short man's friend
the tall man's foe
bringing their reign to an end

it's Death From Below

# JACKIE ROBINSON LEAGUE

by Billy Tuggle

*Heyyy batter! Heyyy batter...*
*SWING!*

90th Street, Tuley Park
Chatter up from around the horn
mimicked across the outfield
WHAP- slap of hand into mitt
while lil' dude at the plate gets the bat
off of his innocent shoulders

*Heyyy batter! Heyyy batter...*
*SWING!*

9-year-old awkward all-star
takes his biggest cut,
barely disturbing the biting breeze,
puts the ball in play
Grey skies battle the sun overhead as
temptation beckons boys on the corner
Seems like there are always runners on the corners

Heyyy batter! Heyyy batter...
*SWING!*

First fly ball of practice, first practice of the season
On the South Side of Chicago,
seasons are not taken for granted
by Black boys who dodge lightning
while trying to bottle and hustle it
"Hustle, Kid, when you cross the lines,"
is not Little League advice anymore.

*Heeyyyy batter...*

If they don't have enough books
at least this kids have gloves
to keep fingers from being idle bait for demons
They learn the power gripping a bat and not a pistol
No live ammunition, this is only a scrimmage
It's Spring and on 90th and King Drive
and little Black boys are singing

*Heyyyy batter! Heyyy batter...!*

# BASEBALL.

by Sam Sax

braiding grass in our city park outfield
tiny inside my big purple shirt, one of my hands

huge and leather. my father's wearing his disappointment
again. his mouth, also leather, stretched thin as a belt.

because i am sitting when all the other boys stand
and because i know how to braid grass this well.

this week, coach lets me throw the ball. he calls me
awful names when it rolls like a belted dog across the plate

so i hit his son with a bat but somehow the blood
spills from my face. this is why i am always in

the outfield. why i imagine green braids roped
in plaits through an empty woman's spun hair.

why my mother bakes with me and lets me pour mud
over her flowers' outstretched hands. she is warm

until it is ten years later, i open myself over the phone
and she breaks like a plate, a ball unstitching, a foul pitcher

of stagnant water. this is when my father finally tightens
his belt and his smile is an open oven howling.

# CURLING HAIR LICKS LIKE FIRE

by Emma Coleman


You snipped long padlocks of curling Irish heritage
From around your freckled face
And now when I get my haircut
Which isn't very often
I think of you
Lift the rustled shavings of iron curls in my empty chest cavity
and remind myself hair is dead as soon as it escapes
the prison that is a body
Best friend, hot winds were pushing your deadness around in waves
Like prairie grasses
And a blade escaped, fleeing the cemetery of your scalp
Like a grave robber
And you gave it to me
Some orange treated keratin
And I put it in mine to see if I could grow hair like yours
And they didn't understand that a 18 year age difference
Didn't mean you were abusing me

I grew fields of orange death to bury myself in
And cried Rapunzel Rapunzel
Cut off your hair
And lend me some so I can be beautiful too
And we can hide in your hair
Together
And eat mangoes
Until our tongues fall out
Then speak in braille on each other's backs
And when our fortress grays
We'll make clouds together
And eat gray things and say gray sayings
And trace gray fingers in the dark air to make gray constellations

Our wrinkles will blend together
Forgetting which one of us was born before the other
We'll just know we have mirror creases
And count our age in chosen nicknames and chosen sisters
We'll use canes together

bleach our linoleum to look like marble
so we sit like sister queens
And when they come to our fortress with torches
The scent of scorched hair, orange death burning like hatred
grandpa beat the interracial couple
daddy hated your gay friend
Like how fire burns wood
And wood smashes skulls
And skulls finally let the death they've pushed out for years
        matte against them
In coagulated scarlet molasses puddles
Like how they've been hurting us for all of time
how we are everyone who has ever been told
some friendships are wrong
This is for our own good
That some death is good

Then the sticks and stones will break my bones
But the heart is a muscle
I don't love you with my femur
Best friend
I love you with my aggravated ziplock silences
And a ventricle with your name on it
In the division of my heart space

Best friend, former teacher
run I'll distract them
Run Best friend
Best friend

Keep running
I use your hair as my armor
Let their armies run army men across my scalp
Spreading napalm
Until my hair is orange too

Your orange looked like fire
Death was on fire
I was on fire
With death on my head
Turn over my body like a new leaf
You'll bury me first
I know it

# SAID THE FLY KILLING ITSELF TRYING TO ESCAPE THROUGH A CLOSED WINDOW, COMPLETELY IGNORING THE OPEN DOOR

by Cristin O'Keefe Aptowicz

Don't worry,
I'm not a metaphor

# "...FAITH IS WHAT YOU MAKE IT..."

by Adam Levin

1.
At my first funeral I was ten.
Faith was a mirage.
It could be broken with a fingertip.
My suit itched. My legs wanted fresh air.
I thumbed the hymnal
and tried to find my name.
2.
In the letters students
have written to children
in the detention center
I remember
"God has not forgotten you."
I catch myself
before something
falls apart.
3.
You've heard a lot about Chicago.
About the bad kids here,
what happens if their stare
cuts through you like tendon
on an empty train car.
When Lamon and I
arrive at the juvenile
detention center, the hallways
are emptied of children.

Usually, there are shoulder
blades in restraint, lines
of students in bruise blue
sweatsuits. Some of them
wear their hair like manes;

others like afterthoughts.
This is where we spent our Thursdays,
in a state of constant leaving.

The best Thursdays are when
I've offered my hand more
than I've hidden it.
When there are ciphers and fists
bouncing from tables that have been
drilled into the floors of their classrooms,
when I smile quickly,
when the guards wonder
what the poems mean,
when every student stays
in the classroom,
when I find out a student
is home and not in class;
when I find out a student
is home and not in class;
when I find out a student
is home and not in jail.

No matter what happy face
you put on what happens here;
that these are bad kids
losing their menace,
we are lying to ourselves.

The counselors are guards;
my students' pods are cells;
these children are prisoners,
pitched headfirst
from the front of a moving train
in the dead of a Chicago summer.

My favorite Bible
story was Jonah.
Some whales
are made
from brick
and steel,
and some oceans
are concrete,
starving for someone
to be spit up.
For so many
of my students
trying to find God,
they have only
to look in their letters
back, itching
through their sweatpants,
legs aching for outside,
where a mirage can
mean they're closer
to the sun.

# CLASS WARPATH

by Jared Paul

It's 2014 and I'm still in the water,
sharks swarm but I'm never swimming for shore,
Let'em Come, Let'em Come! I've sharpened my tongue
Not scared of the deep, ain't afraid to see blood.
Others pulled off the road, headed for home
sunk to the bottom couldn't find a way to float,
low oxygen, closed like a vice up on their throat—
no one hears a scream that can't survive on what it wrote!
But I'm still in the game, castle's on the board
crashing the door, forged Greyhound pass now I'm back on tour,
strapped for war, merch in the bag, food packed, back for more.
Lion in my throat with a fire to feed,
explode out the bottle when the throttle release
small man; sharp teeth. Much dirt undone
and leagues to go before I sleep.

My pops say when you gonna get rich n' make it?
Never! I ain't write the type of stuff that make you famous,
but I get national press for protest arrests;
I *incite* the type of work that might make you famous.
My song is a deep sea alien
that would explode in people's ears
if Payola ever brought it to the surface of a Top 40 playlist
I ain't fakin', it's worth more than they could ever pay me
"Who could own a tree?" like a native,
not gangster, still the FBI hate me
for being that rat, who made it through the maze
and never took the cheese when they gave it.
It's Amazin', I'm AMAZING—
white trash ain't supposed to study wages.
They want us poor, drunk, dumb, and makin' babies,

hooked on sports, god, porn, keep it brain dead
but I made it, out the Matrix,
native healers taught me how to shape shift,
how study race, class, and what the State is.

I know Capital is just exploited labor
and there's a whole lot more but that's the basics.
War is for profit, not national safety,
training youth in genocide for a paycheck.
I found the abyss before I knew what is was
now I can't look away until we break it
but we gonna make it, I can taste it
never been closer to makin' these type of changes.
And I'm afraid but I can't look away
if that's what it takes, man.
Class War till they put me in a jail cell—
but I don't wanna be in no jail cell.

# SUPER VILLAINS...

by Joaquín Zihuatanejo and natasha carrizosa

When I grow up
I wanna' be a Latino Super Villain!
So I can steal from the rich...
and keep that cash for myself.
Because a *vato* can only steal cable for so long
before they flag my house.
My utility belt would be strapped...
with everything a Latino Super Villain needs
to thwart the forces of good
like this thing right here...
a radar detector that can detect the exact location
*of la policia...or la migra!*
or this thing right here
that looks just like a pencil...
okay, it is just a pencil
but if I get right up on you
I can poke your frickin' eye out ese!
Or this thing right here
My secret weapon...
My *Abuelita's chankla!*
We know what you're thinking

*What good can his grandmother's sandal be?*

Believe me,
you do NOT want to taste the wrath of my Abuelita's
       chankla...pen...de...jo!

My arch nemesis...
The Governator

Former Governor Schwarzenegger…this just in…
You are a frickin' immigrant!
How about instead of closing the border
we open your mind.
Drape me a black cape
and don me in an Oakland Raiders football helmet
because my super villain name would be…
Darth Vato
Rising from the depths of my secret underground lair,
that's right ladies…I gotta' lair.
And believe me, I would instruct my minions to
*use the Force…mocosos!*
Because if I were a super villain
I'd be a Latino Super Villain


If I were a Super Villain
I'd be the biggest,
baddest,
colbalt black
super villain
that ever lived.
My name alone would strike fear
into the hearts of men everywhere.
Villainous,
yet rightful,
my super villain name would be…
WOAH-MAN!
I would squirt pure estrogen into the eyes of those
blind to the fact that
that I am stunning…
even without make up.
I don't need no make-up!
You want make up?
Go get freaky with a clown!

And I would be armed
With the all encompassing HALF!
Half of any damn thing a man owns.
I want HALF...
The house
HALF...
The car
HALF...
The dog...

*¿Que?*

I don't care...
Cut that little pooch in two
and give me the half that don't poop on the carpet!
My secret weapon...
the universal doomsday remote control!
And with the push of a button,
your manhood would shrink for every lie you told,
so if by the end of the week
you're singing soprano,
you gots' to go!

*Holla!*

So look out America,
you may just see us as your gentle, wise, tremendously
    underpaid yardman,

or your maid
slash
nanny
slash
mistress
slash yo' tires
slash yo' throat!

But behind these smiling eyes lies a plan

and behind that plans lies us

and behind us lies...

My *Abuelita's chankla!*

*So here we come to wreck the day...*

# BETWEEN HEAVEN AND THE MOST SOUTHERN PLACE ON EARTH

by Aricka Foreman

*for William Foreman Sr. and Emmett Till*


I watch my grandfather's morning fingers slip each button
in then out slotted cotton, sleeves starched to gleam.

Effortless magnolia of a man swaying throughout the house,
limbs bending to his own wind, pooling cologne into his palms,

blessing the edges of jaw, arch of neck, having remembered less
beautiful preparations of the body.  Delta men know how precious

it is to age into the darkness of their own wine, and when his mouth
widens around *darling, I'm so surprised*, it's not the promise of

what a baptism might wash away, but what the 1955 Tallahatchie
River did not. Sometimes I forget which man lives inside my memory,

whose hands lifted me as close to the stars as his shoulders could
reach, making up constellations that didn't ladle the night. I push

against my waking years later to him curled beneath the kitchen
table, folded over and swatting away snakes only he could see,

his howling out writhing from blows his uncle's ghost unleashed
when he was a boy too young to understand why his shade of

gorgeous made people violently uneasy. There are no love songs
for Sunflower, Yazoo, or Money boys to sing to themselves, too few

moments to take in their reflections. They learn to make threading
ritual, pull a string of slow breaths between buffing black

shoes until they catch every fleck of light. When my grandfather pours
into his overcoat, I am young and full of it, not realizing the ease

in which he might not return home before his musk
fades from the front door.

# NOTES FOR MY DAUGHTER AGAINST CHASING STORMS

by Matt Mason

Tornadoes swing through like a kid
playing hopscotch, rip one house to splinters
and leave the neighbors unmussed,
up and down, here and there,
they flatten churches on Easter Sunday,
take up whole towns by the roots,
drive a piece of straw into a tree,
stick a single two by four into a roof
and declare it "art," stack a car
on a car on a motorcycle,
call it a night.

And that, my daughter, is how teenage boys approach love.
I don't say that it is
evil, more like an amoral force of nature,
they look all pleasant showers before they
tear your roof off and leave
your trees in shreds.
So you may dream of his blue
eyes, cloud-free compliments, the music
he likes, the motorcycle he drives,
the great tattoos on his neck, but

when the skies turn that yellow, that green,
when the hail starts popping through air
fit to boil, you listen
to my forecast, you leave the car
parked, grab a flashlight
with one hand, a blanket with the other, go
for the basement, now you run.

# TO THE BOYS WHO MAY ONE DAY DATE MY DAUGHTER

by Jesse Parent

To the boys who may one day date my daughter:

I have been waiting for you.
Since before her birth,
since before my spark took hold
and ignited the fire in her mother's belly.
I have been training
to kill you.

When you took your first steps,
I was preparing to make it
so you never walked again.
When you played at war
I was perfecting headshots.
You can't catch up at this point.

When you meet my daughter
and fall in love with the look she sends over her shoulder,
her crescent moon eyes
framing her laughing smile,
you are going to want to talk to her.
And when the hours pass by like sprinters
during your first timeless conversation
you will also know, with a deep unspoken dread,
that you will have to talk to me.

When you first come to my home
and see the bone carving over my threshold
try not to imagine your own femur so expertly carved.
Pay no attention to my ample crawlspace,

my room with the rubber mats and a drain.
Be careful only to approach me
with love for my daughter.

I have been seeding her childhood
with tap root hugs to weed out indifference and apathy.
There will be no daddy issues
for your teenaged talons to latch upon.

If you break her heart, I will hear it snap
with the ear I pressed against her mother's belly.
The crook of my elbow where I cradled her head
will send a message to my fist.
My cheeks are attuned to her lips,
I will know if they tremble.

I have taught her that a man should never hit a woman.
Her mother would add
that you really shouldn't ever hit anyone,
But I have taught her
that a man should NEVER HIT A WOMAN!
Consider my genes a mark of Cain,
you will suffer seven times over whatever you do to her.
She will not keep your secrets.
You can't make fire feel afraid.

I have tried to teach her love all her life,
All I ask is that you continue the lesson.
Love her, befriend her, protect her.
Be there when I can't.
And when my body gives up to the grave
let the grin eternity carves into my face
be a reflection of the peace your love brings to her,
and we should get along just fine.

## ADDENDUM

To the girls who may one day date my daughter:

My wife is a better shot than I am.

# NEBULA

by Hakim Bellamy


*In the middle of a high school parking lot*
*in the middle of the day*
*in the middle of Arizona*

they stand
pointing at the sky
like it stole something

like a vending machine
that is a quarter klepto
and there they are
empty handed at the altar of it

pointing at a refund
getting nothing in return

so I ask them
what are you pointing at?

as the sound barrier
breaks their give-a-damn
into pieces and pity
they say, "stars"

and I say…
"Where?"
*as I stand in the middle of a high school parking lot*
*in the middle of the day*
*in the middle of Arizona*

and they say, "can't you hear them?"
that star is called Apache
named for my ancestors, I think?
it means "enemy"
a name we've inherited
along with generations of this sky
on the brink of smoke and steel

then I say, "Well, what's that star, then?"

and they reel them off
like rounds

Harrier,
B–52
F–15

and I point one hand at them
like they are lying
then put the other over my mouth
like I am too

"What's that star?" I say
"We call it Blue Angel." They say

F/A-18 Hornet
says Messier

my mouth behind my hand
is still open
wishing I could catch one of these fireflies
insulting planets and impersonating stars
take them out, trash-like
stop the sound of them circling us
like we are a pile of...

if these are their stars
I am terrified to see their gods

though the sky
is not the only thing above them
that they cannot reach
it is the bluest

every hair on their little heads
counted and crossed
wishing, God
wasn't the armed, silent type

pointing their futures
towards the big vending machine in the sky

standing
*in the middle of a high school parking lot*
*in the middle of the day*
*in the middle of Arizona*

pointing at stars
that point back.

# COMIC BOOK ME.

by Rob Sturma

If you were to draw me in a comic book,
I would have a collar around my neck
and the leash attached would be held by my heart.
It'd be a cartoony heart, more like a valentine
and less like a fist.   It would wear dark glasses,
not because it was blind, but because it was
sensitive.   It would lead me headfirst into
many, many wacky adventures.

I think most of my ex-girlfriends would concur
that this would be a most accurate hieroglyph.

I grab a big gooey ball of caution,
determine which way the wind is blowing,
and then throw that caution directly into its breezy path.

Sometimes it splatters back into my brave face.

But Comic Book Me would wipe that goop off of his glasses
and wear the rest down his cheeks
like warpaint,
like he was the Ultimate Warrior of Love.

Somedays I have so much saccharine
in my delicate platelets
that Care Bears develop diabetes in my presence.

Comic Book Me walks down the street
as if drawn by a magnet
shaped like a witty turn of phrase.
He is not fooled by siren songs

as he is too busy listening for seventeen syllables
that sound like *forever I'm yours.*

He goes in for a routine physical
and the x-ray reveals
a sap factory in his guts.
A library in his lungs.
Arrested development in his cynicism gland.

I sketch Comic Book Me onto napkins
and cash register paper. He seems
so small, so pure. He is a blob of a man,
all glasses and ears and unfading smiles.

As I fall asleep, I turn down the word balloons
emanating from the television box,
make sure all the borders of my panels
are tucked in, and take sheep inventory.

Their soft bleats rise and fall
as I dream of a world
where Comic Book Me finds his muse,
a winged mermaid who sings to him
of a hopeful man constructed out of
creaky flesh and deep sighs. Comic Book Me
pledges to help this carbon-filled golem
find his purpose. There will be, he vows,
the happiest of endings. It is a story
that I can invest in and believe


as I wait anxiously for the next issue.

# THANK YOU:

Thanks to the teachers who believed in the first book and encouraged me to do another especially Missy Hughes, Dave Stieber, Hiu To, Lydia Merril, Kent Martin, Peter Kahn, Amanda Cordes, and the teaching artists at Young Chicago Authors.

Tim Stafford is a poet and public school teacher from Lyons, IL. He was the 2007 Chicago Grand Slam Champion and has appeared on the HBO series Def Poetry Jam. He performs regularly at festivals all over the U.S. and Europe including the Louder Than A Bomb Teen Poetry Festival, the 2008 Brecht Festival (Germany) the 2010 Zurich Poetry Slam Festival (Switzerland), the 2011 German National Poetry Slam, the 2013 Kiel Wochen Festival (Germany), and the 2014 Woerdz Festival (Switzerland). He lives in Willow Springs, IL with his son Mikey, and his dog, Betsy.

For updates on performances or to contact Tim, visit www.learnthenburn.com

Photo Credit: Uwe Lehmann, www.photographiemanufaktur.de

# IF YOU LOVE LEARN THEN BURN,
## LEARN THEN BURN LOVES . . .

*Oh, Terrible Youth*
by Cristin O'Keefe Aptowicz

*These are the Breaks*
by Idris Goodwin

*Courage: Daring Poems for Gutsy Girls*
by Karen Finneyfrock, Mindy Nettifee & Rachel McKibbens, Editors

*Spiking the Sucker Punch*
by Robbie Q Telfer

*Learn Then Burn Teacher's Manual*
by Tim Stafford and Molly Meacham, Editorsy

Write Bloody Publishing distributes and promotes great books of fiction, poetry, and art every year. We are an independent press dedicated to quality literature and book design, with an office in Austin, TX.

Our employees are authors and artists, so we call ourselves a family. Our design team comes from all over America: modern painters, photographers, and rock album designers create book covers we're proud to be judged by.

We publish and promote 8 to 12 tour-savvy authors per year. We are grass-roots, D.I.Y., bootstrap believers. Pull up a good book and join the family. Support independent authors, artists, and presses.

**Want to know more about Write Bloody books, authors, and events?
Join our mailing list at**

## www.writebloody.com

WRITEBLOODY
QUALITY AMERICAN BOOKS

# WRITE BLOODY BOOKS

*After the Witch Hunt* — Megan Falley

*Aim for the Head, Zombie Anthology* — Rob Sturma, Editor

*Amulet* — Jason Bayani

*Any Psalm You Want* — Khary Jackson

*Birthday Girl with Possum* — Brendan Constantine

*The Bones Below* — Sierra DeMulder

*Born in the Year of the Butterfly Knife* — Derrick C. Brown

*Bouquet of Red Flags* —Taylor Mali

*Bring Down the Chandeliers* — Tara Hardy

*Ceremony for the Choking Ghost* — Karen Finneyfrock

*Clear Out the Static in Your Attic* — Rebecca Bridge & Isla McKetta

*Courage: Daring Poems for Gutsy Girls* — Karen Finneyfrock, Mindy Nettifee
& Rachel McKibbens, Editors

*Dear Future Boyfriend* — Cristin O'Keefe Aptowicz

*Dive: The Life and Fight of Reba Tutt* — Hannah Safren

*Drunks and Other Poems of Recovery* — Jack McCarthy

*The Elephant Engine High Dive Revival* anthology

*Everyone I Love Is A Stranger To Someone* — Anneleyse Gelman

*Everything Is Everything* — Cristin O'Keefe Aptowicz

*The Feather Room* — Anis Mojgani

*Floating, Brilliant, Gone* — Franny Choi

*Gentleman Practice* — Buddy Wakefield

*Glitter in the Blood: A Guide to Braver Writing* — Mindy Nettifee

*Good Grief* — Stevie Edwards

*The Good Things About America* — Derrick Brown and Kevin Staniec, Editors

*The Heart of a Comet* — Pages D. Matam

*Hot Teen Slut* — Cristin O'Keefe Aptowicz

*I Love Science!* — Shanny Jean Maney

*I Love You is Back* — Derrick C. Brown

CPSIA information can be obtained at www.ICGtesting.com
Printed in the USA
LVOW07s0024200115

423493LV00003B/22/P